MARITIME GREENWICH

THE OFFICIAL SOUVENIR GUIDE

This edition published by National Maritime Museum Enterprises Ltd, 2011,
on behalf of the Maritime Greenwich World Heritage Site Partnership

National Maritime Museum
Greenwich
London SE10 9NF
www.nmm.ac.uk

ISBN: 978 1 906367 53 4

Original text (1999 edition) by John Bold and
Charlotte Bradbeer (English Heritage),
and Pieter van der Merwe (NMM)
This edition revised and re-edited
by Pieter van der Merwe

Project managed by Lara Maiklem and Diana Christou
Designed by Nigel Soper
Photography by Tina Warner and David Westwood (NMM)
Production Management by Geoff Barlow

Printed in the UK by Belmont Press

10 9 8 7 6 5 4 3 2 1

Maritime GREENWICH
A WORLD HERITAGE SITE

FRONT COVER:
Greenwich in the 1740s from John Rocque's 'Exact Survey of the Cities of London and Westminster...' (1746). PBC5317

Contents

This guide is mainly to help you find you way around historic Greenwich. It only briefly summarizes the main heritage attractions (for which there are other guidebooks); the gazetteer adds more, keyed by number to the map in the back cover, and also includes locations in the Information for Visitors section.

HSBC

Introduction

WELCOME TO MARITIME GREENWICH, inscribed as a World Heritage Site by UNESCO in 1997. There are more than 500 such sites in over 100 countries. Some are natural wonders, others are man-made, but all have this international status because of their outstanding importance and universal value.

Maritime Greenwich includes the historic town centre and Royal Park, the Old Royal Naval College, Ranger's House and the three sites comprising the Royal Museums, Greenwich: the Queen's House, Royal Observatory and National Maritime Museum. Many of the buildings are by the greatest British architects of the seventeenth and eighteenth centuries, and as a group they form a unique historic townscape.

Greenwich was the site of a major royal palace from the mid-fifteenth century on: Henry VIII and Elizabeth I were born there. From 1676 Charles II's Royal Observatory made it a centre of pioneering work for the improvement of navigation and, later, global time-keeping. The Royal Hospital for Seamen, begun in 1696, was a national institution for maritime welfare before it became the home of the Royal Naval College (1873–1998), and today it is a modern university campus. Greenwich was therefore the ideal site for the National Maritime Museum, opened in 1937, and for the preservation of the *Cutty Sark*, the last and most famous of the tea-clippers, which arrived in 1954.

All this and much more is here for you to enjoy. The story of the World Heritage Site is briefly told in the Discover Greenwich Visitor Centre at the Old Royal Naval College. This is housed with the Greenwich Tourist Information Centre, close to the Pier and *Cutty Sark*.

This guide will help you discover Maritime Greenwich as a whole, with further sources of information at the end. Much more – and links to the various attractions – also appears on our website www.visitgreenwich.org.uk, so visit that too to stay in touch.

The Queen's House, with the Old Royal Naval College and the Canary Wharf towers behind, from Greenwich Park.

A Place in History

On Thames's bank in silent thought we stood,
Where Greenwich smiles upon the silver flood:
Struck with the seat that gave Eliza birth,
We kneel, and kiss the consecrated earth.

Dr Samuel Johnson (lived in Greenwich, 1737)

WHEN DR JOHNSON wrote this in 1738, Greenwich was a riverside village on the fringe of London, but already had a long history. Strategically placed next to the main land and water routes from continental Europe to the capital, it was one of the main bases for the Danish conquest of England in the early eleventh century. The site of a small Roman shrine on the east side of the Park and a cluster of Anglo-Saxon burial ground mounds on the west show even older occupation.

Greenwich Hospital, painted by Canaletto at about the time of its completion in 1751, with the Queen's House, Park and distant Observatory. BHC1827

BELOW: **Time from Greenwich**. 'H4', John Harrison's prize-winning timekeeper of 1759, which finally solved the problem of fixing longitude at sea. ZAA0037

In Johnson's time, its main activities were centred on the Royal Naval Hospital, founded in 1694 and replacing the former royal palace where King Henry VIII and Queen Elizabeth I were born. Of this, the only surviving building is Inigo Jones's Queen's House, completed about 1638. The Hospital was home to the blue-coated and battle-scarred Pensioners of the Royal Navy until 1869.

It then served from 1873 as the Royal Naval College and, in addition from 1983, as the Joint Services Defence College, both for advanced officer training. Both colleges moved to Shrivenham, Wiltshire, in 1998.

These buildings beside the Thames, with the Royal Observatory crowning the first of all London's royal parks behind them, form the finest architectural landscape in Britain. The Observatory itself was founded by Charles II in 1675, expressly to improve the seaborne navigation on which the wealth and security of Britain depended. It did this by accurately mapping the stars, for which accurate time measurement was critical: since 1884 the world has also set its clocks according to time on the meridian of Greenwich, Longitude 0°, the baseline of the International Time Zone system.

Nowhere else in Britain has so many outstanding buildings designed by our foremost classical architects. The town centre also bears the imprint of over 300 years of growth and adaptation, and still largely preserves the elegant Georgian domestic and commercial buildings it had gained by the 1840s. Until the Thames became badly polluted in the late nineteenth century, whitebait swam upriver as far as Greenwich and were a local delicacy, attracting celebrities and others to such inns as the surviving Trafalgar Tavern, and The Ship, which once stood where the most beautiful of sailing vessels, *Cutty Sark*, now stands in dry-dock – newly and spectacularly restored.

The kings and queens, the Pensioners, Samuel Pepys, Dr Johnson, Nelson, Dickens and others – famous and unknown – have gone; but they would still easily recognize the Park, the great buildings and the bustling urban scene. The once-busy river, now much cleaner, is also slowly becoming busier again. Historic Greenwich has largely survived: an island in the city, where the story of Britain and the sea, and of time itself, can be enjoyed in a unique architectural and landscape setting.

BELOW: **Time at sea.** 'K2' Larcum Kendall's second, simplified version of Harrison's 'H4', which was issued to Lieutenant Bligh in 1787 for his ill-fated *Bounty* voyage. It went with the ship and the *Bounty* mutineers to Pitcairn Island and ended up in Chile, before being presented to Captain Herbert of HMS *Calliope* in 1840, for return to England. ZAA0078

Royal Greenwich

GREENWICH HAS HAD ROYAL CONNECTIONS for 600 years, a history celebrated in 2012, when it formally becomes a Royal Borough to mark HM The Queen's Diamond Jubilee. It was a royal manor from at least the fourteenth century, when a new Thames-side house called Bellacourt was built here by Humphrey, Duke of Gloucester, regent from 1426 to his nephew, the young King Henry VI. In 1433 Humphrey fenced in 200 acres (81 ha) of heath, woodland and pasture to form the Park, and built a watchtower where the Observatory now stands. After his death in 1447, Bellacourt passed to Margaret of Anjou, wife of Henry VI, and was renamed Placentia, while 'Duke Humphrey's Tower' was later remodelled as a lodge by Henry VIII, who housed one of his mistresses there.

Placentia, in turn, was largely rebuilt by Henry VII around 1500 and became the Palace of Greenwich. Until the building of Whitehall Palace in the 1530s, it was a principal Crown residence, not least as the first (or last) port of call for visiting ambassadors from mainland Europe. Henry VIII, a compulsive builder and an enthusiastic horseman and jouster, made further alterations during his reign (1509–47). He redesigned the chapel, remodelled stables and added a tiltyard with towers and a viewing gallery. Martial displays, in which he played a vigorous part, became highlights of diplomatic and other such events, marked by jousts, banqueting, the performance of masques and dancing until dawn. It was also here that Henry established his

BELOW: **'Fayre Greenwich Castle'**, by Wenceslaus Hollar, 1637. Duke Humphrey's Tower as remodelled by Henry VIII and under James I, overlooking Greenwich Palace. PAJ2421

RIGHT: **Henry VIII**, a portrait after Holbein. BHC2763
FAR RIGHT: **Elizabeth I**, British school, *c.*1590. Both Henry and Elizabeth I were born at Greenwich and used it as a main residence. BHC2680

OVERLEAF: **'A View of the Ancient Royal Palace called Placentia, in East Greenwich'**; an engraving by James Basire taken from a drawing in the Bodleian Library. The towers on the left are those flanking the tournament yard behind the Palace. PAH3294

armoury (the first of its kind in England) and, nearby, his two great naval dockyards – at Woolwich to the east and Deptford to the west.

When Whitehall supplanted it as the leading seat of Tudor government, Greenwich became a royal country retreat. Henry VIII's daughter Elizabeth, who spent most summers here, maintained the banqueting houses and added a new one in 1559, but did little other building. Under King James I, the courtier Earl of Northampton (d. 1614) revamped Duke Humphrey's Tower

as the ornamental castle of Millefleur, complete with a kitchen, wine cellar and private garden. At the same time James replaced the fence around the Park with a brick wall approximately 2 miles (3.2 km) in length and 12 feet (3.5 m) high, at a cost of about £2,000. In the Palace, he added a stone-vaulted undercroft beneath the Great Hall and built new lodgings for his wife, Anne of Denmark.

Shortly afterwards he assigned the Palace to her, and she began improvements, among which was her greatly admired Italianate garden. Devised by the French garden designer and hydraulic engineer, Salomon de Caus, with fountains, water-pouring statues, an aviary and a shell-encrusted grotto, it appeared so artfully natural that, according to a French visitor, 'it seems that art had hardly any part'. Anne's final innovation was to have Inigo Jones design the Queen's House in 1616, overlooking the gardens. Building stopped before she died in 1619 and it was ten years before her daughter-in-law Queen Henrietta Maria resumed it, both reviving the gardens and bringing the House to usable completion by about 1638.

Greenwich and London from One Tree Hill, by Johannes Vorsterman *c.*1680. The painting shows the Queen's House, the incomplete wing of Charles II's new palace, the Observatory and the ruins of the Tudor Palace. BHC1808

After the Restoration of King Charles II in 1660, the dilapidated Palace was gradually demolished as part of his plan to replace it with a modern classical structure of three ranges open to the river. This was designed by John Webb, a pupil of Jones, but money problems ensured that only one of these ranges was begun in 1664. Boarded up in 1669, still incomplete, it was used as a gunpowder store until Queen Mary II decided to incorporate it into her new hospital for seamen in 1694. Charles's intentions for the Park were comparably ambitious. A plan survives that was prepared by the great French garden

designer, André le Nôtre, creator of the parks at Versailles and Vaux-le-Vicomte, although it was only partly executed. It was mainly implemented by Sir William Boreman, who planted many of the tree-lined avenues and, in 1661–62, cut the Giant Steps that linked the upper and lower parts of the Park. Four of these are still visible on the eroded slope up to the Observatory. At the south end of the Park, the major and minor avenues radiated from a semicircle of trees flanked by contrived wildernesses, one of which – the Great Wilderness – survives as a small area of woodland. Still hidden inside it is an enclosure for a herd of deer, which Henry VIII first introduced in 1515–18, and which ran free in the Park until the 1920s.

The Queen's House

Designed by Inigo Jones, this Italianate 'house of delight' is one of the most important buildings in British architectural history, representing the pure classicism that Jones introduced to England in the service of the Stuart court. Work began in 1616 for James I's queen, Anne of Denmark (1574–1619), but stopped in 1618 when it was only one storey high. Queen Henrietta Maria (1609– 69), wife of King Charles I, resumed construction after 1629 and was still engaged on lavish interior furnishing at the start of the Civil War in 1642, which destroyed the Stuart idyll, resulting in the King's execution and the Queen living in exile until 1662.

The House was created by Jones as a small-scale version of a Renaissance villa, and as a private retreat for the Stuart queens, based on extensive study of architecture and gardens in Italy. His specific model was the Medici villa of

BELOW: **The House from the north**. Jones may have intended this façade to have painted decoration, as a permanent backdrop for welcoming important visitors on the terrace. Eighteenth-century sashes now replace the original leaded mullion-and-transom windows.

RIGHT: **Inigo Jones (1573–1652)**.
Little is known of Jones before he gained fame as a designer of court masques. The Queen's House, begun for Anne of Denmark and completed for Henrietta Maria, is his most influential building. This is Hogarth's version of a portrait by Van Dyck. BHC2810

RIGHT: **The House from the Park**. The south side with the first floor loggia is the main façade, providing an elevated view over the Park. The House originally opened directly into it. The present wall and 'ha-ha' ditch (originally to exclude deer but now planted as a border), date from the early nineteenth century.

Poggio a Caiano, outside Florence, by Giuliano da Sangallo. Instead of Sangallo's central salon, however, Jones designed the House as a bridge over the Deptford to Woolwich road, which then divided the palace gardens from the Park: it replaced an earlier Tudor gatehouse that had also performed this function.

Thus in essence, the house was two separate buildings, linked by a single central room over the road at first-floor level. At the time it was rightly regarded as a 'curious device'. The addition of two further bridge rooms in the 1660s has partly obscured this original 'H-plan', turning the building into a more conventional square, while the road itself was moved north to its present position in about 1699.

The House has had a chequered history, remaining in the ownership of the Crown but being occupied by various people including the Ranger of Greenwich Park, a post held in the early eighteenth century by the Governor of the Royal Hospital (to 1743). It was also used as a place for receiving royal visitors to England, including George, Elector of Hanover, before his

OPPOSITE: **Anne of Denmark (1572–1619)**. James I's queen in a portrait by John de Critz. Although she died shortly after it was begun, the Queen's House was part of a programme of improvements to stamp her identity on Greenwich, after James granted her the manor in 1613. BHC4251

ABOVE: **Royal Pair**. A Van Dyck studio portrait of Henrietta Maria, with her husband, Charles I, after Van Dyck. BHC2761, BHC2607

coronation as George I in 1714, and a number of later royal brides. From the early nineteenth century it housed the Greenwich (later Royal) Hospital School, before being restored from 1934 as centrepiece of the new National Maritime Museum.

The cubic, galleried, two-storey hall, the dramatic Tulip Stairs and the plasterwork of the early 1660s bridge rooms, as well as the view of the Park from the loggia, give a flavour of the grandeur intended by the royal occupants. Much of the decorative painting commissioned by Henrietta Maria remained incomplete, however, and many artworks that were installed were dispersed after the execution of Charles I in 1649. Orazio Gentileschi's original ceiling paintings in the Hall, forming an 'Allegory of Peace and Arts under the English Crown' were removed to Marlborough House in about 1708 but the Queen's Bedchamber still has the original ceiling coving painted in 'grotesque-work'. This is probably by Matthew Gooderick, who also worked at Somerset House.

OVERLEAF: **The Tulip Stairs**. The first centrally unsupported spiral stair in Britain. Its name derives from the pattern of the wrought-iron balustrade. The stairs originally led from the ground floor to a polygonal turret on the roof.

Today the Queen's House is one of the three sites that comprise the Royal Museums, Greenwich, and displays the National Maritime Museum's superb art collection. It is also used for some temporary exhibitions, and for corporate and private events, which distantly echo its likely original court functions. Through its style, position and status, the Queen's House also determined the form of all later developments on the palace site, including the 'Grand Axis' from the River up through the Park. For when built, it had no view to or from the Thames: that was only gained with the demolition of the old Palace in the 1670s, and both Charles II's plans for a new one and Sir Christopher Wren's original design for the Royal Hospital would have blocked it again. This was stopped by Queen Mary II, who, in founding the Hospital, reserved an open strip of ground the width of the House to form a 'visto' to and from the river. Admiral Sir William Gifford, the first Governor of the Hospital, was an early beneficiary: in 1712 he ordered two oak seats for the terrace, from which to enjoy the view.

BELOW: **Art in the Queen's House**. The House is now used to display aspects of the National Maritime Museum's art collection. Shown here are portraits of Admiral Lord Rodney by J.-L. Mosnier, Lady Hamilton by Romney, Nelson when a young captain by J.F. Rigaud *(see p.70)* and the Canaletto view of Greenwich *(see pp.6–7)*.

The Old Royal Naval College

THIS MAGNIFICENT GROUP OF BUILDINGS was largely constructed between 1696 and 1751 as the Royal Hospital for Seamen, mainly to the designs of Sir Christopher Wren and Nicholas Hawksmoor. Like the earlier Royal Hospital at Chelsea, which is still a grand almshouse for army veterans, 'Greenwich Hospital' was for Royal Naval seamen who were unable to maintain themselves for reasons of age or disability. The first Greenwich Pensioners arrived in 1705, the last left under new welfare arrangements in 1869, and from 1873 to 1998 the buildings housed the Royal Naval College, 'the Navy's university'. The finest piece of monumental classical architecture in England, the College holds two masterpieces of interior decoration:

BELOW: **The twin domes** of the Old Royal Naval College, rising over the exterior of the Painted Hall, seen from the western end of College Way.

ABOVE: **Greenwich Pensioners on Trafalgar Day, 1835**, watercolour by S.P. Denning after John Burnet's painting of 1837, which was bought by the Duke of Wellington. Those shown include Nelson's servant Tom Allen (holding his portrait, left), men from the crew of *Victory* at Trafalgar and boys from the Greenwich Hospital School. PAJ2612

Sir James Thornhill's Baroque Painted Hall and the Neoclassical chapel, as rebuilt by James Stuart and William Newton after a fire in 1779 gutted Thomas Ripley's plainer original one.

The College stands on the site of the former Tudor Palace of Greenwich. Its earliest visible section is the east side of the King Charles Court, which was the start of a new palace for Charles II in the 1660s. When Queen Mary II decided that this and the rest of the site be 'converted and employed as a hospital for seamen', she also decreed that the Queen's House retain a view to the river, which it did not originally have: this explains the unusual arrangement of paired buildings each side of a central 'visto'. She died of smallpox in December 1694 and her husband William III continued the project in her memory, promising

ABOVE: **'The Pensioner's Story'**, by Thomas Davidson. Visitors to Greenwich listen to a Pensioner's yarn. BHC1815

an endowment of £2,000 a year. Sir Christopher Wren, formally appointed Surveyor in 1696, worked free of charge. He was assisted by Nicholas Hawksmoor, who in 1698 became Clerk of Works (a post he held until 1735) and by John James, assistant to Hawksmoor from 1705 and later joint Clerk with him. Sir John Vanbrugh was a member of the Board of Directors from 1703 and followed Wren as Surveyor from 1716, but had little part in the design. The main lines of the Hospital, including all of the foundations, were laid out by Wren. The 'courts' were designed by him and Hawksmoor with the exception of the last, the Queen Mary Court, although this outwardly mirrors its domed Wren 'pair' (King William Court).

Despite the promising start, the project was bedevilled by financial difficulties, with construction spread across four main phases, between 1696 and 1751, and with further improvements being made into the nineteenth century. By 1699 the scheme was £9,000 in debt, and this had grown to £19,000 by 1702. It was only in 1735, when the Hospital was granted the northern estates of the Earl of Derwentwater (who was executed for supporting the Jacobite rising of 1715), that it gained the steady income which allowed Thomas Ripley, a reliable rather than outstanding architect, to begin the Queen Mary Court. Given the problems, however, it is remarkable that the Hospital was completed at all, let alone in such splendid style.

Significantly, Hawksmoor later referred to Queen Mary's 'fixt Intention for Magnificence' when she founded it. For while such hospitals were designed to fulfil the welfare obligations of monarchs to support men disabled in serving their country, they were also overt demonstrations of state power, wealth and benevolence. Given Britain's position as a leading maritime nation, building her Royal Naval Hospital on the river highway connecting London with

ABOVE: **Pensioners dining**. When Thornhill began decorating the Painted Hall in 1708, dining for the Hospital Pensioners was moved to the undercrofts below the Hall and the Chapel, remaining there until the Hospital closed. PAI8790

the world was as much a political as a philanthropic act. This was underlined by the spectacular decorative scheme in the Painted Hall, which launched Greenwich as an international visitor attraction from 1712, when Thornhill finished the main ceiling. The voluntary charge to view it was soon made compulsory, and from about 1715 allowed the Hospital to found what became the Royal Hospital School for the sons of seamen. In 1824, partly to keep up charitable profile and income in the years of peace after the Napoleonic War, the Hall became the 'National Gallery of Naval Art' (or Naval Gallery), eventually housing over 300 paintings – all donated to the Hospital – and attracting thousands of visitors a year. The first 'national historical gallery', this contained many famous naval paintings and relics, especially relating to Nelson. It lasted until 1936 when, as the Greenwich Hospital Collection, it crossed Romney Road into the care of the new National Maritime Museum.

IAM NOVA PROGE

LEFT: **The Upper Hall**. The less familiar part of the Painted Hall, originally intended as the Hospital officers' dining area. Queen Anne, the last of the Stuart dynasty, looks down from the ceiling with her husband Prince George of Denmark, above the spot where Nelson's body lay in state after his death at Trafalgar in 1805. On the left, *en grisaille* and in classical guise, William III (Willem of Orange), Anne's predecessor and husband of her elder sister Mary II, lands at Torbay in 1688 to overthrow their father James II. On the right George I (as Elector of Hanover and great-grandson of James I) lands at Greenwich in 1714 to succeed Anne, following her death without a direct heir. The Latin legend across the top of the 'great west front' proclaims the Hanoverians as 'a new race in heaven' with George I and his family beneath.

OVERLEAF: **Greenwich from the river**. The 'Canaletto' view of the Royal Naval College and the Queen's House.

CAROLVS II REX

OPPOSITE: **The Chapel**. The marble floor is laid to a nautical cable pattern, and the pulpit is the top section of the original 'three-decker', which used to stand centrally in front of Sir Benjamin West's altarpiece depicting 'St Paul after shipwreck on Malta' (1789).

The first 46 Pensioners arrived in 1705 and there were 1,000 by 1738. At most, in 1814, the Hospital housed 2,710 'in-Pensioners', with several thousand others who (from 1763) drew 'out-Pensions' to support themselves either locally or elsewhere. The capacity of the buildings was expanded, particularly in the more space-efficient Queen Mary Court (1735–51). Construction of a dedicated infirmary in the 1760s – now the Dreadnought Building – also made more space during a period of worldwide naval conflict.

With such numbers, two sittings for meals were needed in the two colonnaded dining rooms (each with its own kitchen) beneath the Chapel and Painted Hall, which was only used for dining on special occasions. The Pensioners' diet was plain and repetitive: mutton on two days a week, beef on three, with pea soup and cheese on the other two. Two quarts of beer a day were provided, which was piped to the dining areas from the Hospital's own brewhouse. Smoking was limited to specific places, especially after it was blamed for the 1779 Chapel fire: latterly this was in the Chalk Walk, a long basement under the east colonnade, which eventually became a skittle alley. A Pensioners' library was only added in 1828 and even by 1860 the First Lord of the Admiralty, the Duke of Somerset, regretted that most Pensioners passed their days 'in a state of listless idleness and mental vacuity, until recalled at fixed intervals to their meals or their beds. It is not surprising that old sailors so circumstanced should resort to the alehouse or worse places.'

BELOW: **Wren to Regency**. The western range of the King Charles Court was Wren's first addition to the eastern part built in the 1660s. It was remodelled in its present Regency form by John Yenn in 1812–15.

OPPOSITE: **The King William Courtyard**. Pensioners in the courtyard, as seen by James Holland, *c.*1850. The cobbled courtyard undulates strongly in a pattern designed to help drainage. The Pensioner in a yellow jacket with red sleeves is a 'canary' – a defaulter obliged to wear this punishment dress, confined to the Hospital and to doing menial chores for disciplinary reasons. BHC1832

Demand for places also declined in a long mid-nineteenth-century era of naval peace, and in 1860 a Commission of enquiry recommended that the Hospital close. Most remaining Pensioners left in 1865 with annuities to support themselves outside, and the last 'helpless' cases had gone into other care by 1869. In 1873 the Admiralty transferred its Naval College, established at Portsmouth in 1841, to form the Royal Naval College at Greenwich, 'for the education of officers of all ranks above midshipman in all branches of theoretical and scientific study bearing on their profession'. In 1983 the Joint Services Defence College also arrived.

In 1998, following the Government's 1995 decision to move both service training facilities elsewhere, responsibility for the College passed to the Greenwich Foundation, a charitable management trust specially formed to ensure the appropriate care and use of the site, and to encourage public access and appreciation. The main buildings are now occupied by the University of Greenwich, and the King Charles Court by Trinity Laban Conservatoire of Music and Dance. The Foundation has overall responsibility for the College, the Painted Hall, the Chapel and the grounds.The Discover Greenwich Visitor Centre is in its Pepys Building, adjacent to Greenwich Pier and the *Cutty Sark*, and is also home to the Greenwich Tourist Information Centre.

RIGHT: **The Discover Greenwich Visitor Centre** and the Greenwich Tourist Information Centre are located in the Pepys Building. The Visitor Centre explores more than 500 years of history through its permanent display, which includes historic exhibits, film footage, hands-on displays, and dressing-up costumes.

The Royal Observatory

SINCE 1884, the world has set its clocks according to the time of day on the meridian of Greenwich, Longitude 0°, which is defined by the Airy Transit Circle installed at the Royal Observatory in 1850–51. This was a development from the Observatory's original purpose, which was set out when Charles II appointed John Flamsteed as his first Astronomer Royal in 1675, instructing him, 'to apply himself with the most exact care and diligence to the rectifying the tables of the motions of the heavens, and the places of the fixed stars, so as to find out the so much-desired longitude of places for the perfecting the art of navigation'. At that time Britain was a rising sea power, and finding accurate longitude (east–west position) in mid-ocean was the greatest of many navigational problems. It would remain so for over 80 years, since it could only be done by accurate time measurement. North and south position (latitude) was relatively easy by observation; but instrumentation and charts also needed improvement and all involved accurate celestial data.

Flamsteed House is the original Observatory building, designed in 1675 by Sir Christopher Wren with the advice of Robert Hooke, and built on the foundations of Duke Humphrey's Tower/Greenwich Castle. The site had the advantages of being on (then-secluded) royal ground, near to London but outside its smoky haze, and also high up with clear fields of view. Cost was also saved by building on the old tower foundations, although this put the new walls about 13½° out of north–south alignment, making them unsuitable to mount transit instruments on.

Designed, in Wren's words, 'for the Observator's habitation … and a little for pompe', Flamsteed House had domestic accommodation on the lower floors, with the Star Room, now called the Octagon Room, above it. This was large and grand enough to welcome VIPs, and to accommodate long telescopes and two specialized clocks. These were built for Flamsteed by Thomas Tompion and installed in 1676, each with a 13-foot (4m) pendulum for accurate time reckoning. They required winding only once a year and enabled Flamsteed to establish that the Earth rotated at an even rate, giving him a basis

Flamsteed House. The original Royal Observatory building, constructed in 1675–76, partly of recycled materials, and paid for by the sale of decayed gunpowder. It cost £520 9s 1d.

ABOVE AND LEFT: **The Octagon Room**. Originally called 'the Star Room' when it was first engraved in 1676 by Francis Place, this was more for important visitors than day-to-day observing. The portraits set above Tompion's vital year-going clocks in the panelling are of Charles II and James II. ZBA1808

RIGHT: **Bradley's Meridian**. Troughton's 10-foot transit telescope of 1816 set up on the 1750 Greenwich meridian defined by the third Astronomer Royal, James Bradley. This is still the basis of British land maps but is about 19 feet (6 m) west of the modern Prime Meridian.

for precisely charting the stars by timed observations of their transit (crossing a meridian) over his head.

It was in the shed-like Quadrant House – just to the south of the present Meridian Building – that Flamsteed did his main work. Here he was able to mount his transit quadrant on a wall that ran truly north–south and first define a 'Greenwich Meridian'. The official meridian later moved east four times as subsequent Astronomer Royals set up ever more accurate transit instruments in eastward extensions of what is now the Meridian Building, ending with that defined in 1851 by George Biddell Airy, seventh holder of the post (1835–81). In 1857 Airy also added the octagonal Great Equatorial Building as a telescope tower, although in 1892–93 its original drum-shaped top was replaced by a larger onion dome for the 28-inch (71cm) refracting telescope of 1894. This onion dome was removed in 1953 after being damaged in 1944 by a near miss from a V1 flying bomb, which left still-visible scars on the base of Wolfe's nearby statue. It was replaced by a fibreglass replica in 1975, when the telescope was also returned after thirty years' use on the later working Observatory site in Sussex.

LEFT: **The first 'sea-clock'.** John Harrison's first large timekeeper 'H1' was completed in 1735. He finished his perfected prototype 'H4' in 1759 *(see p. 8)*. ZAA0034

ABOVE: **John Flamsteed**, from a portrait by Thomas Gibson. Born in 1646, Flamsteed was appointed first Astronomer Royal at Greenwich in 1675 and died still in-post in 1719. His 44 years of charting the heavens were the foundation of all subequent work at Greenwich. ZBA0744

RIGHT: **The Greenwich Meridian**. When the Observatory was still a closed scientific site, the public could only see a line marking the Longitude 0° meridian outside, below the courtyard railings.

OPPOSITE: **Domes of heaven**. The Altazimuth Pavilion, 1899, which now holds a photo-heliograph for observing sunspots, and the 28-inch (71cm) Great Equatorial telescope dome. The wind-vane of Halley's Comet is copied from the Bayeux Tapestry.

RIGHT: **The statue of Major-General James Wolfe**, whose capture of Quebec in 1759 brought Canada into British hands, has overlooked Greenwich since it was presented by the Canadian people in 1930.

BELOW: **An eighteenth-century sea-compass** in the collection at Greenwich. NAV0027

The Meridian Building provides a sober contrast to picturesque Flamsteed House, but expansion under the eighth Astronomer Royal, William Christie, was more decorative. With the architect William Crisp he designed the Altazimuth Pavilion and South Building – originally the 'New Physical Observatory' – both erected in 1894–99. The Pavilion originally held a telescope on an altazimuth mounting, enabling movement on both north–south (altitude) and east–west (azimuth) axes. The much larger South Building was built in phases to 1899 and reopened in May 2007 as a public astronomy centre, after total internal remodelling. The centre also includes the striking 120-seat Peter Harrison Planetarium, under a new raised courtyard and truncated bronze cone. The design of the cone takes into account its location in relation to the zenith, the north celestial pole, the celestial equator and the meridian.

SHEPHERD PATENTEE
LONDON
CLOCK
THE SHEPHERD 24-HOUR GATE CLOCK
THE TIME BALL
ORDNANCE SURVEY BENCH MARK
PUBLIC STANDARDS OF LENGTH
BRITISH YARD
TWO FEET
SIX INCHES
THREE INCHES

OPPOSITE: **The 24-hour Shepherd Gate Clock** of 1852 at the Observatory, the first clock to show Greenwich time to the public, as it still does.

RIGHT: **Sir George Biddell Airy** (1801–92) was seventh Astronomer Royal, 1835–81. From 1852 he transformed 'Greenwich time' from a nautical and scientific concept to a fully public one, by using the new electric telegraph to transmit it from the Observatory. This portrait of him in his warm observing coat is by John Collier. BHC2507

ABOVE: **Maria Belville (1811–99)**, the first 'Greenwich Time lady'. Maria was the third wife and widow of John Henry Belville, who began delivering 'Greenwich Time' to London clockmakers in 1836. Maria continued this to 1892 and was more famously succeeded by their daughter, Ruth, who did so until 1940. All used a pocket chronometer that Ruth called 'Arnold', the name of its maker. PAI8786

City pollution, the building of Greenwich Power Station in 1902–10, and the disturbing effects of electric railways on magnetic observations, obliged the Observatory to move aspects of its work elsewhere from the 1920s on. World War II accelerated this and, afterwards, all scientific work moved to Herstmonceux Castle, Sussex. The Astronomer Royal left in 1948, although positional observations continued at Greenwich until 1954, a year after the buildings were allocated to the National Maritime Museum and became known as the Old Royal Observatory. The

Octagon Room was opened to the public in 1953 and, in July 1960, Queen Elizabeth II opened the restored Flamsteed House, the complex being fully reopened in 1967. Ironically, the 'Royal Greenwich Observatory' (as the scientific body was known at Herstmonceux and later at Cambridge) finally closed in 1998 and, although certainly 'old', the Royal Observatory, Greenwich, has now reassumed both this title and the RGO's educational role in modern astronomy. With the Museum and Queen's House, from January 2012 it became one of the three sites collectively renamed the Royal Museums, Greenwich.

BELOW: **Planetarium and the South Building**, The bronze cone of the Peter Harrison Planetarium, with the 1899 South Observatory behind. The latter provided accommodation for the scientific departments of the Royal Observatory and held a telescope in the roof dome until 1967, when the space was turned into the Caird Planetarium. The new planetarium opened in 2007, following a major redevelopment.

ABOVE: **Figure representing Astronomy**. The South Building's elaborate terracotta decoration includes the names of famous astronomers and instrument makers, with a bust of John Flamsteed over the entrance.

LEFT: **The Time-Ball**, installed on Flamsteed House in 1919, replacing the first one of 1833, drops at 1 p.m. It was originally used by ships in the Thames to set their chronometers.

OVERLEAF: **The Queen's House** at Christmas time, with the laser beam marking the Greenwich Meridian northwards from the Observatory seen behind it.

Cutty Sark

THIS BEAUTIFUL TEA CLIPPER, the fastest ship of her time and the last survivor of her type, is preserved in dry-dock at Greenwich as a tribute to the ships and men of the Merchant Navy in the days of sail, and as a testimony to London's distinguished maritime past. Built of teak on an iron frame by Scott and Linton, *Cutty Sark* was launched at Dumbarton in Scotland in 1869. Ironically the same year saw the opening of the Suez Canal (for steamers only), which spelt the end of the high-value sailing trade in tea for which *Cutty Sark* was built. After 1877 she transferred to the Australian wool run, on which she really made her name, principally under the command of Captain Richard Woodget between 1885 and 1895. Immensely strong and powerful, she was famous for overhauling both sailing and steam vessels, the most celebrated of many occasions being in 1889, when she overtook the new P&O mail steamer *Britannia* on the run into Sydney. On Woodget's first voyage in 1885, she defeated her old tea-trade rival *Thermopylae* on the voyage from Sydney by a full week, arriving off the coast of Kent after 73 days at sea.

From 1895 *Cutty Sark* was in Portuguese hands as the *Ferreira*, but was bought back in 1922 by Captain Wilfred Dowman of Falmouth. In 1938 she came to Greenhithe on the lower Thames as a training ship for the Thames Nautical Training College. When no longer needed for this purpose, the Cutty Sark Preservation Society, formed in 1952, with HRH The Duke of Edinburgh as patron, ensured her survival. The ship was moored off Deptford as part of the Festival of Britain in 1951. In 1954 she was moved into her dry-dock, which was built at cost by Sir Robert McAlpine, and after three years of restoration was opened to the public by HM The Queen. The ship is now run by a reformed Cutty Sark Trust and has recently undergone massive further restoration to ensure her long-term survival.

***Cutty Sark* statistics**
Tonnage – 963 tons
Sail area – 32,000 square feet (2,987 square metres)
Best day's run – 363 nautical miles
Highest measured speed – 17.5 knots

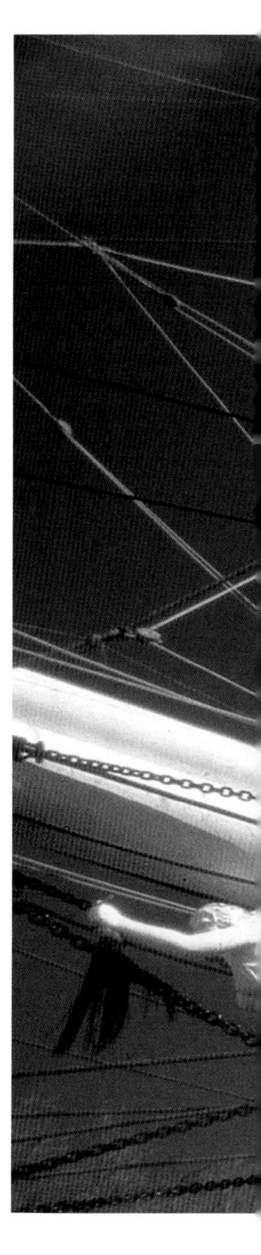

'Weel done, cutty-sark!'. The ship's figurehead is the witch Nannie from Robert Burns's poem 'Tam O'Shanter', wearing the 'cutty sark' (short shift) of the story. She is grasping the tail of Tam's horse, torn out in her pursuit of him.

CUTTY SARK

CUTTY SARK

Restoring *Cutty Sark*, 2006–12

After fifty years in her Greenwich dry-dock, *Cutty Sark*'s structure had badly deteriorated as a result of rainwater ingress and complex, long-term corrosion processes in her wrought-iron frame. In November 2006 a major new conservation programme began to counter the metal decay and consolidate the wooden hull planks. Originally projected at about £25 million, costs increased by a further £10 million when a major fire affected the ship in May 2007, although luckily it involved little loss of original fabric. Generous Heritage Lottery grants, both before and after the fire, and other grants and donations have helped meet the funding needs. In June 2008 a gift of £3.3 million from a shipping magnate, Sammy Ofer, completed the essential restoration target, but fundraising has continued to help ensure the ship's long-term sustainability. The re-opening was originally planned for 2010, but will now take place in 2012, with *Cutty Sark* permanently raised over 10 feet (3 metres) and surrounded by a dramatic glass canopy covering her dock. This design will allow the space underneath the hull to be used for interpretation of the ship and her history, and for other public and private events. For more information, please visit www.cuttysark.org.uk.

OPPOSITE: **'Where There's a Will is a Way'**. The stern decoration of *Cutty Sark* (around the large letter 'W') includes this motto of John 'White-hat' Willis, the flamboyant merchant for whom she was built.

RIGHT: ***Cutty Sark*** lying at Deadmen's Buoys, Deptford, during the Festival of Britain in 1951. She was moored there for visitors to come aboard at the start of the campaign for her long-term preservation. The old Deptford Power Station is on the right with Greenwich beyond.

OVERLEAF: ***Cutty Sark* at sunset**, by John Everett. This is one of many images of the ship by Everett, a marine painter who voyaged the world under sail while *Cutty Sark* was still at sea. BHC3278

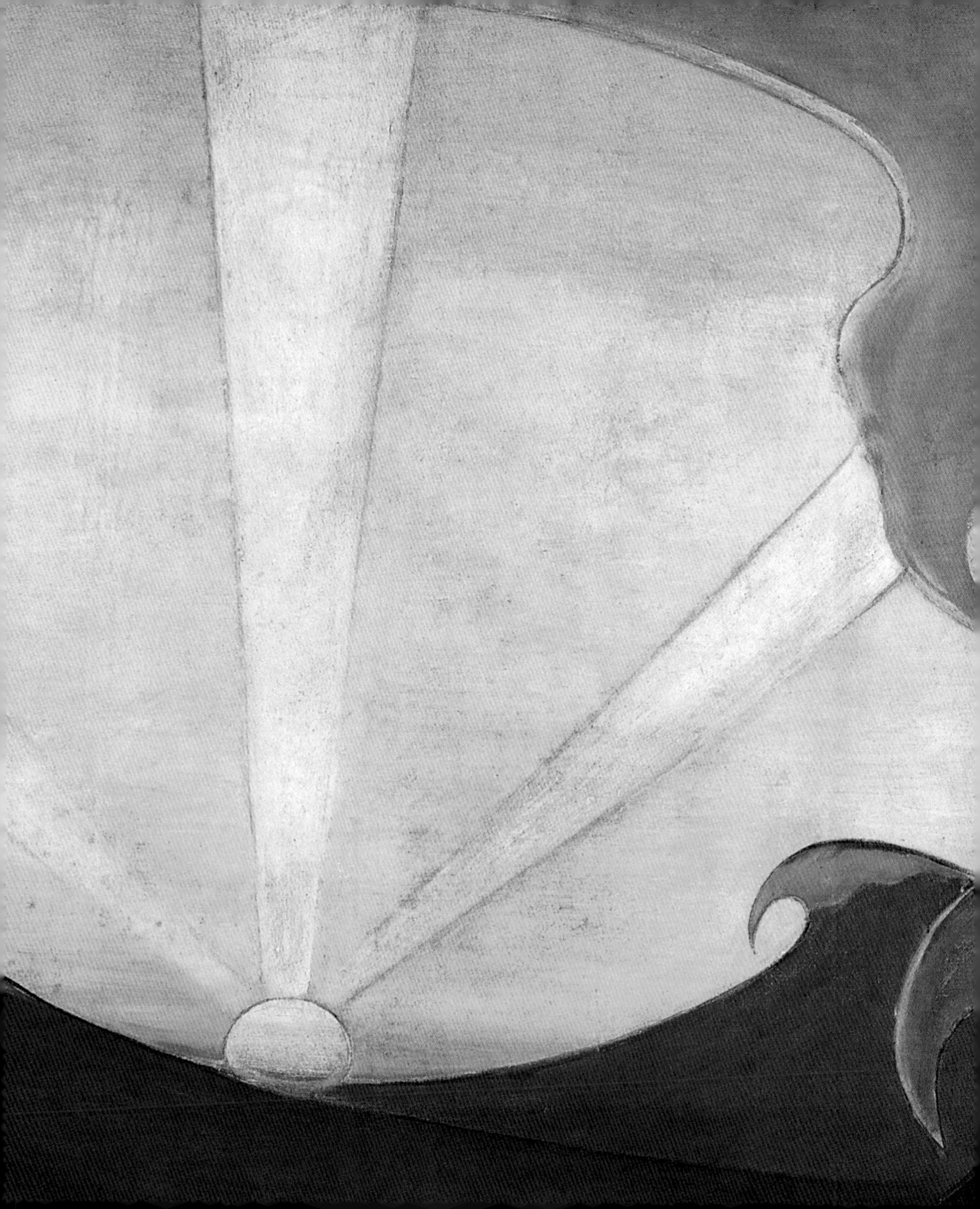

The National Maritime Museum

THE NATIONAL MARITIME MUSEUM at Greenwich is the largest of its type in the world. It is the 'flagship' of the three Royal Museums, Greenwich, with the Queen's House and Royal Observatory also under its command, and its maritime collections are unequalled in terms of both quality and size. They tell the story of Britain and the sea, navigation, and the measurement of time and space. Although primarily historical, the displays also cover modern issues such as global warming, the continuing importance of sea trade and the sea as a focus of leisure and cultural interest. The Museum holds 2.5 million items, of which the vast majority are documents or images on paper for research purposes, as opposed to objects for display, but only a small proportion in either category can be shown at any time. There are more than 4,000 oil paintings, 70,000 prints and drawings, 2,500 models, 3,300 instruments, 50,000 sea charts, 100,000 books, 1 million photographs, 750,000 ship plans and 25,000 'antiquities', as well as 1.5 miles (3 km) of shelved manuscripts. It also has more than 100 boats, most of which are

BELOW: **Map of the World after 1492**, coloured engraving by Francesco Rosselli, about 1508. This map has meridians and parallels drawn for every 10° and is surrounded by heads, representing the twelve winds. G201:1/53

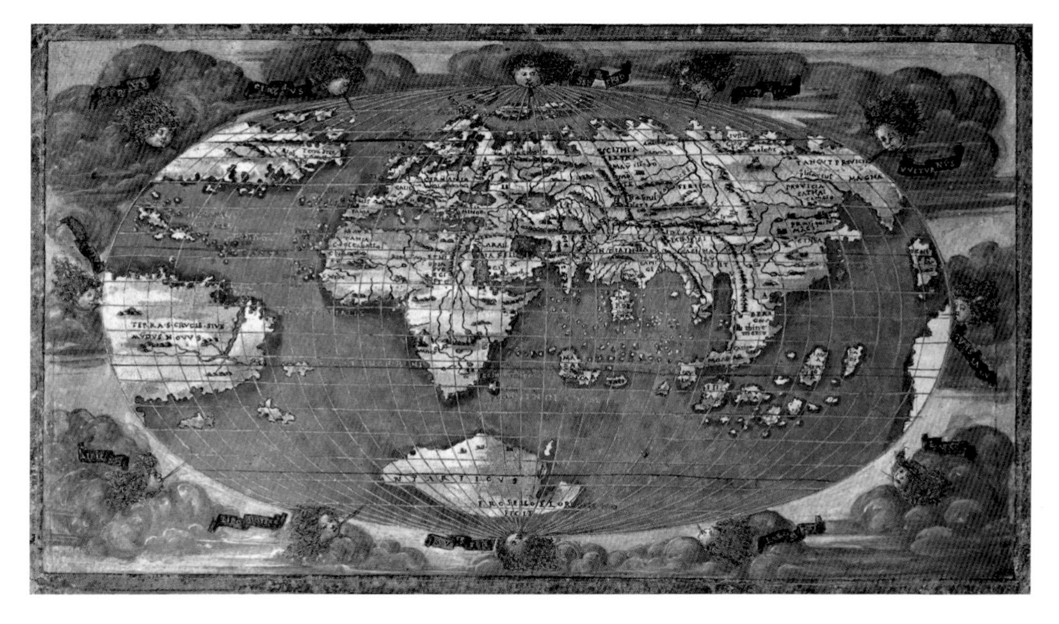

ABOVE: **The North Entrance**. This imposing façade, the Stanhope Entrance, dates from 1873 and is named after the Museum's founding Chairman. It is now the dedicated entry for large organized groups. The area behind, Neptune Court, was totally redeveloped, from 1996 to 1999.

displayed at the National Maritime Museum Cornwall, which opened on the Falmouth waterfront in 2002.

Aspects of the Museum holdings are enormously famous. It has the world's finest collections on the Royal Navy in the era of sail, and in particular on Nelson and his times; the same is true in many areas of navigational and related scientific instruments, including John Harrison's celebrated marine timekeepers, which finally solved 'the longitude problem'. The art collection is also unparalleled, comprising both the finest single collections of Dutch seventeenth-century and later British marine paintings, and England's largest collection of portraits other than that housed in the National Portrait Gallery. The Caird Library is the largest maritime historical library and archive in the world, with various items dating back to the fifteenth century.

While some of the collections themselves go back centuries, the Museum was founded by Act of Parliament only in 1934, and opened in the Queen's House and adjoining buildings in 1937.

The two inner wings were added to the House in 1807–11 to convert it into a school – the Royal Naval Asylum. This was established at Greenwich by

Royal Warrant in 1805 to accommodate 700 boys and (until 1841) 300 girls, and was quite separate from the Greenwich Hospital School, which educated 'orphans of the sea' from 1715.

The architect of these extensions was Daniel Asher Alexander, after he suggested that 'the architect be directed to form his plan in strict accordance with the style of Inigo Jones'. He was immediately given the job and produced a very sympathetic result, including the fine colonnades that served as covered play areas for the children.

The Asylum was taken over by Greenwich Hospital in 1821. Combined with its own school as the Upper and Lower Schools of Greenwich Hospital, it was organizationally reformed and extended with a south and outer west wing in 1861–62, designed by Philip Charles Hardwick. In 1873 an iron-vaulted gymnasium known as 'Neptune's Hall' was added between the two west wings, behind the imposing Doric façade that now forms the Museum's north entrance. A large dining hall and dormitory wing were the final additions on the west side in 1876, and the whole complex was renamed the Royal Hospital School in 1892.

'England Expects ...'
J.M.W. Turner's painting of *Victory* at the Battle of Trafalgar was commissioned by George IV. The only painting by Turner in the Royal Collection, it proved so controversial that the King gave it to Greenwich Hospital in 1829. BHC0565

After the school moved out to Suffolk in 1933, the buildings were converted to house the new Museum, largely at the cost of Sir James Caird (1864–1954), a Scottish shipowner who was its greatest early benefactor. He had already been the main private backer in preserving Nelson's flagship *Victory* at Portsmouth, and eventually put over £1.25 million into acquisitions and buildings for the Museum, working with its Trustees and first Director, Sir Geoffrey Callender: this sum would be well over £100 million in today's terms. During the conversion a top-lit rotunda by Sir Edwin Lutyens was inserted into Alexander's west wing, honouring Sir James. The Greenwich Hospital collection of paintings, displayed in the Painted Hall of the Royal Naval College, and material from the former Royal Naval Museum there, were transferred to the new Museum's care in 1936. The Observatory buildings were added in the 1950s.

ABOVE: **Brass-framed sextant**, by Jesse Ramsden of London, made in 1772 and used on Captain Cook's third Pacific voyage, 1776–80. NAV1236

OPPOSITE: **Sailor suit**, made on board the Royal Yacht for the six-year-old Prince of Wales (later King Edward VII) in 1846. It started a fashion which still endures in civilian clothing. UNI0293

IMPLACA

Neptune's Hall was used for the royal opening by King George VI in 1937, and afterwards it became a display area for boats, models and other large objects until 1972, when it was redesigned as the new 'Neptune Hall' with the 1907 paddle-tug *Reliant* as a centrepiece. This lasted until 1997, when the entire Hall was dismantled in a £20-million Lottery-funded redevelopment by Rick Mather Architects and the Building Design Partnership. The façade remains but behind it a vast atrium, the 'Neptune Court', now forms the centre of the Museum, beneath a glass and steel roof that spans the whole area between the 1807–62 west wings.

While this project and related new gallery displays made the Museum much more 'visitor-friendly', various practical problems remained, not least inadequate space for major temporary exhibitions and to increase public access to the library and archive collections. This resulted, in 2008, in a plan to add a new wing and a new main entrance on the Park side, to improve the link with the Park and Royal Observatory. As the issue of finding the £30 million to do this was being addressed, the Museum was offered £20 million, the largest single benefaction yet given to a British museum. The donor was Sammy Ofer who, though born in Romania, had served in the Royal Navy during the Second World War and later built up an international shipping business. Designed by C.F. Møller and Purcell Miller Tritton, the new Sammy Ofer Wing was opened in July 2011 by HRH The Duke of Edinburgh (the Museum's Patron,

LEFT: ***Implacable* in Neptune Court**. The stern of the last 74-gun ship of the line, originally the French *Duguay-Trouin*, which fought at Trafalgar in 1805 and was captured shortly afterwards. Later a training ship at Portsmouth, she survived until 1949 but was then beyond saving. The Museum stored the 'gingerbread work' of her stern for over fifty years until it was possible to display it.

and formerly its longest-serving Trustee). The visibly new low-profile Portland stone extension includes both a new entrance and visitor facilities, with an 8,610 sq foot (800 m^2) international-standard special exhibition gallery at basement level. Less obviously the project included the complete internal conversion of the adjacent South-West Wing of 1876, changing three floors into four, to hold a new introductory gallery for the Museum at entrance-floor level, with an enlarged reading room and two-and-a half-floors of library and archive storage space above. The terrace roof of the new wing holds a brasserie and offers a fine view over the Park, from which it is separated by a new garden area including water features.

ABOVE LEFT: **Captain Sir John Franklin** (1786–1847), in a photograph taken just before he led the 1845 expedition to the North-West Passage on which he, his two ships and, all 128 men who accompanied him were lost. 9191–1

ABOVE RIGHT: **Sir Walter Ralegh** (1554–1618) was an important early promoter of exploration. This terracotta bust of 1757 is by John Michael Rysbrack. SCU0043

OPPOSITE: **Captain James Cook** (1728–79) in a portrait by William Hodges, the artist on his second Pacific voyage of 1772–75. BHC4227

OVERLEAF: **Blackwall Yard**, painted by Francis Holman in 1784. On the north side of the Thames just downstream from Greenwich, this was then the biggest commercial shipyard in the world, building large merchant vessels and warships for the Navy. The one being launched here on the left is probably the 44-gun *Adventure*. Ship repairing only ended on the site in the 1980s. BHC1866

Captn James Cook
of the Endeavour.

WILLIAM IV

LEFT: **King William IV** 'the Sailor King' (r. 1830–37), with the Museum's Sammy Ofer Wing in the background. Samuel Nixon's statue of 1844 originally stood in the City of London but was moved to Greenwich in 1936 – luckily to a position where it was possible to design the Museum's new main public entrance from 2011 around it. It is made of two blocks of Devon granite with a total weight of 45 tons (41 tonnes).

ABOVE: **Old and new**. The Museum's South-West Wing of 1876, now holding the new Caird Library and archive, reflected in one of the roof lanterns of the Sammy Ofer Wing.

OPPOSITE: **'I will be a Hero'**. John Francis Rigaud's portrait of Nelson shows him as a young captain in 1781. BHC2901

RIGHT: **Admiral Lord Nelson's** undress uniform coat at Trafalgar in 1805. By the time he wore this he had lost his right arm and was loaded with decorations. The fatal bullet hole is in the left shoulder. UNI0024

The Thames and the Town

In its item 'Holiday Walks', the *Penny Magazine* in 1832, recommended travelling to Greenwich by water: 'the domes and colonnades ... will rise from the shore, and impress your mind with a magnificence of which the architecture of England presents few examples'. This was shortly before London's earliest suburban railway reached Greenwich in 1836–38. For centuries the River Thames was the principal and easiest route, and the approach by river remains equally dramatic today. One certainly best appreciates the full extent of the historic heart of Greenwich from a boat in mid-stream or from Island Gardens on the north bank: the eye is led from the riverside courts of the Old Royal Naval College to the central Queen's House and up to the Royal Observatory on the hill. The riverside walk terminates to the east with the Trafalgar Tavern and to the west with the masts of the *Cutty Sark*, standing close to where the main landing place for Greenwich has always been.

The historic town now has the late-Georgian appearance given to it by Joseph Kay, then Surveyor to Greenwich Hospital. He re-planned the town centre in the late 1820s, with the intention of separating the Hospital from it and providing a grand approach to its gates. Supported by the Hospital's Secretary, Edward Hawke Locker, Kay wished to improve the 'circuitous, narrow and unsightly' road route from London, which was further blighted by an open-air market. His scheme cleared away the decayed post-medieval town that pressed up against the Hospital boundary, and replaced it with a formal layout of commercial streets around a new covered market, built in 1829–31. Originally, this had three principal sections, for meat, fish and vegetables. Above the colonnaded entrance from College Approach there is still a biblical exhortation to fair trade: 'A False Balance is Abomination to the Lord but a Just Weight His Delight'.

Today, the fresh produce has gone, replaced by craft and antique stalls, under a glazed roof installed in 1908. By 2014 the utilitarian commercial buildings around this will also be replaced. The parades of stuccoed terraces designed by Kay compare favourably with contemporary schemes in the West End of London. He was responsible also for the elegant Trafalgar Tavern, whose cast-iron balconies, canopied bow-windows and an upper-storey loggia give fine views over the Thames. It was built on Royal Hospital land in 1837,

St Alfege's Church, by Nicholas Hawksmoor, 1711–14, and consecrated in 1718, though the tower of the previous church is hidden inside the 1730 remodelling by John James. It marks the reputed spot where Vikings murdered Alfege, Archbishop of Canterbury, in 1012.

replacing the old 'George' tavern. Kay was not above abusing his personal influence, for the new lease was granted to his brother, John, rather than the leaseholder of the 'George'.

The architectural focus of Greenwich is Nicholas Hawksmoor's remarkable church of St Alfege, a replacement of 1711–14 for the medieval church whose roof collapsed in 1710: St Alfege was Archbishop of Canterbury, murdered on the site in 1012 by Danish raiders camped at Greenwich. This was the first of the 'Fifty New Churches' in London ordered under Queen Anne. Twelve were built, six of them by Hawksmoor and one by John James, his colleague at the Royal Hospital. James was also responsible for recasing the surviving medieval tower of St Alfege in 1730. The church was damaged by World War II bombing in the 1940s and its interior sensitively restored by Sir Albert Richardson in 1953.

A Seaman's Town

Greenwich was always a place of river workers, fishermen and seamen. From 1705, when the first 46 naval Pensioners entered the still largely incomplete Royal Hospital, it also came to be a Royal Naval town. As the all-male 'in-Pensioner' complement increased – apart from some seamen's widows employed as nurses – wives and families came to live near their men, and Hospital 'out-Pensioners' and other seamen also settled locally. Wives took in washing or worked as servants or in shops. Pensioners, distinctive by their uniform, disabilities, seamanly bearing and nautical speech, thronged the narrow lanes, took the air in the Park and for a small coin or tobacco regaled goggle-eyed holiday visitors with tales of great battles, exotic foreign lands, and storm and shipwreck on distant oceans.

BELOW: **'Battles by Sea and Land'**. A Greenwich and a Chelsea Pensioner swap yarns in a print of 1801. PAD4733

Greenwich was a place of inexpensive and often licentious pleasures, with its riotous twice-yearly fair (to 1857), its pot-houses and its taverns. The carved balconies of 'The Salutation' hung over the landing place – for many trippers came by water from London. 'The Ship' was also on the Thames, off narrow Fisher Lane behind the modern pier. Pictures, stories and song celebrate the Pensioners and show them carousing in such haunts, refighting old battles over foaming tankards and long clay pipes. For once 'safely moored in a Greenwich berth', their main enemy was boredom: the Hospital looked after them well, but it was strictly run and they had few occupations – not even a reading room until 1828.

Those who broke the Hospital rules were called 'canaries', and were made to wear a yellow coat and perform menial tasks, until this humiliation was abolished by Nelson's old flag-captain Sir Thomas Hardy when he was Governor of the Hospital, 1834–39. In fact, many Pensioners were disabled men who were quite young, and some lived to great ages, often over 100. One man who had been servant to Admiral Byng when he was executed in 1757 was still telling his tale after 1800. The last survivor of the loss of the *Royal George* off Portsmouth in 1782 died in 1840, and John Roome, the signalman who hoisted 'England expects' for Nelson at Trafalgar, died here in 1860.

RIGHT: **'Fisher's Alley'**. A watercolour by Clarkson Stanfield of the lane that ran towards the Hospital behind modern Greenwich Pier. It was demolished around 1840. PAJ1960

The Park and its Borders

GREENWICH PARK today still has some of the strong formal lines of its seventeenth-century layout, but overall it is more a landscape park of the eighteenth century. It has been open to the public since about 1705 but only on a regular basis from the 1830s when it became locally notorious for 'improper' holiday behaviour by visitors. Set around the Park are some of the best surviving examples in London of affluent private houses of the seventeenth to nineteenth centuries. Within it there are various monuments and buildings of note, as well as Roman and Anglo-Saxon remains. Among the trees, the great chestnuts, some dating from the 1660s' layout, are especially fine.

Apart from having the Observatory at its summit, Greenwich Hill has always offered fine views of the historic buildings below it and of distant London. Many artists have taken advantage of this. Well-known seventeenth-century views by Danckerts and Vorsterman were followed in 1809 by the greatest of English landscape and marine painters, J.M.W. Turner, and by later nineteenth-century recorders of both the landscape and the Park social scene. Westwards the eye is led along the Thames towards the dome of Sir Christopher Wren's St Paul's Cathedral – a view now legally protected from intrusion from the

OPPOSITE: **Ranger's House**. The main part was built *c.*1700 for Admiral Francis Hosier. The writer and statesman 4th Earl of Chesterfield who later lived here, added the south gallery. In June 2002 the House became home to the superb Wernher Collection, particularly notable for its Renaissance *objets d'art*. This is the rear of the house, overlooking the fine rose garden that now backs it in Greenwich Park.

RIGHT: **'The Great Wilderness'** was the seventeenth-century name of a large unlandscaped area in the south-east corner of the Park. What remains of it is now the enclosure for deer: Henry VIII introduced them to the Park and they roamed free until confined here in 1927.

spread of ever-taller and more dominant modern buildings. East and north lie surviving points of river-based industry and the Richard Rogers Partnership's O2 (the former Millennium Dome). In front, the cluster of large, modern Docklands buildings has grown ever-denser around Cesar Pelli's still generally superior Canary Wharf tower (1 Canada Square), which was completed in 1991.

In 1835 the young Charles Dickens recorded his impressions of Greenwich Fair. For over a hundred years this was one of London's great popular attractions at Easter and Whitsuntide: 'a periodical breaking out ... a sort of spring-rash: a three day's fever, which cools the blood for six months afterwards, and at the expiration of which, London is restored to its old habits of plodding industry'. The principal day-time amusement observed by Dickens, 'is to drag young ladies up the steep hill which leads to the observatory, and then drag them down again, at the very top of their speed, greatly to the derangement of their curls and bonnet-caps' (*Sketches by Boz*).

An earlier observer had noted rather more than derangement. In 1730, 'great numbers ... diverted themselves ... with running down the Hill ... one of them, a young woman, broke her Neck, another ran against one of the Trees with such Violence that she broke her Jaw-bone and a third broke her leg.' When night fell, the action moved to the town where itinerant theatres, menageries, objects of curiosity like dwarfs and giantesses, and a temporary ballroom, vied for the attention of enormous crowds; all, as Dickens wrote, 'was primitive, unreserved and unstudied'.

Such excess met opposition as the age became increasingly prim, and as annual numbers at the two fairs rose to about 250,000 with the coming of both steam ferries and trains to Greenwich in 1836–38. In 1857, after thirty years of complaint, respectable local residents succeeded in abolishing the Fair, which the *Greenwich Free Press* called, 'that old market of vice and debauchery'. Greenwich has been a tamer place since but the Park still has few equals as one of 'the lungs of London'.

The Observatory's dominance in the Park can make one overlook other interesting structures, such as the cast-iron, pagoda-like bandstand of 1891 and the delightful teahouse of 1906–07. To the south, at the Blackheath Gate, is John Phipps's lodge of 1851–52, a remarkably early example of the Domestic Revival style; to the north, by the road gate to the town, is the stuccoed St Mary's Lodge of 1807–08, designed by John Nash as an Italianate version of a picturesque estate lodge. Across the road, and now the centrepiece of the new

ABOVE: **The flower gardens** in the south-east corner of the Park enclose the deer reserve behind them.

south entrance to the National Maritime Museum, is Samuel Nixon's granite statue of King William IV, the 'Sailor King'. Erected at the City end of London Bridge in 1844 it was moved here in 1936, onto what was then the site of George Basevi's recently demolished St Mary's Church (1823). Other notable monuments include Robert Tait McKenzie's bronze statue (1930) of General Wolfe, who lived beside the Park, died at Quebec in 1759 and buried in St Alfege's. A Henry Moore abstract bronze *Standing Figure, Knife Edge* was placed on the hill west of the Observatory in 1979 but had to be removed later for practical reasons. It made a welcome return in autumn 2011.

Maze Hill, to the east of the Park, and Croom's Hill to the west, offer a rich variety of styles in historic houses. Begun in 1718, Vanbrugh Castle, on Maze Hill, was built by the architect and playwright Sir John Vanbrugh as his own residence in a dramatically medievalizing style, recalling the vanished Duke Humphrey's Tower/Greenwich Castle. Other properties of note on the hill

OVERLEAF: **Aerial view of Greenwich**, 2008. This clearly shows its position relating to the great southern loop of the Thames around the Isle of Dogs, with the towers of Canary Wharf at the top. Note the visiting cruise liner lying on the deep-water mooring between Greenwich and Deptford. Due north and south (the Greenwich Meridian) is a line from the Observatory, lower centre, narrowly slicing across the tip of the Greenwich Peninsula (Blackwall Point) to the north, upper right.

include numbers 32–40, built by Daniel Asher Alexander in 1807–12 as the infirmary of the Royal Naval Asylum (later combined with the Greenwich Hospital school) but ultimately divided into five houses. Its site had been Greenwich Hospital's first burial ground, of which the enclosing walls and an officers' mausoleum survive.

Croom's Hill, the ancient route to Greenwich from Blackheath, has one of the finest concentrations of seventeenth- and eighteenth-century houses in London. The largest are at the top on Chesterfield Walk: Macartney House and the Ranger's House. Parts of the former (Wolfe's family home) date from the late seventeenth century, with 1802 extensions by Sir John Soane. The adjacent classical Ranger's House was built around 1700 for Admiral Francis Hosier, best remembered by a ballad *(Admiral Hosier's Ghost)*, which marked his death from fever in the West Indies. In 1815, after some earlier additions, it became the 'grace and favour' residence of the Ranger of Greenwich Park: now run by English Heritage, it holds the spectacular Wernher Collection of fine and decorative art, much of which dates back to the Renaissance.

Further down the hill are late-seventeenth- and early eighteenth-century houses and terraces. The Manor House (*c.*1700) near the top is particularly

ABOVE: **Tumbling on the Hill**: 'At Greenwich lies the scene, where many a lass / Has been green-gowned upon the tender grass…' (William Mountfort, 1691). A traditional and sometimes dangerous pastime on the hills of Greenwich Park, notorious for creating 'sweet disorder in the dress' of pretty girls. From an engraving published about 1770. PAH3277

OVERLEAF: **View of Greenwich and the Thames from the Park**. An anonymous early eighteenth-century view, about 1735, with ships moored off Deptford Dockyard in the middle distance and St Paul's Cathedral beyond. BHC1834

BELOW: **The 02** (formerly the Millennium Dome). The Greenwich Peninsula has become Europe's largest area of inner city regeneration. Its centrepiece is the Dome – designed by the Richard Rogers Partnership. Twelve 328-foot (100-m) masts support the tensioned glass-fibre canopy which is 1,247 feet (380m) across, making it Europe's largest single-span covered area. Having housed Britain's controversial 'New Millennium Experience' through the year 2000, the Dome, renamed the 02,is now a 20,000-seat arena for sporting and musical events, and part of the ongoing redevelopment of the area.

fine, and the seventeenth-century Grange has a splendid garden-wall gazebo overlooking the Park. This was designed by Robert Hooke in 1672 for the owner, Sir William Hooker, Sheriff and later Lord Mayor of London. The most imposing building on Croom's Hill, the Gothic Revival Roman Catholic Church of Our Lady Star of the Sea, was built of ragstone in 1851 to the designs of William Wardell, later an important architect in Australia. On the northern boundary of the Park, houses on Park Vista include the last standing remnant of the Tudor palace, a conduit house of about 1515 bearing the arms of Henry VIII. This is now part of a group of seventeenth- to nineteenth-century houses: The Chantry, (no. 34) and St Alfege's Vicarage. Eastward, across the road, the early eighteenth-century Manor House has an unusual weather-boarded belvedere. This overlooks the Park's walled former 'Dwarf Orchard', the last survivor of three seventeenth-century tree nurseries along its northern edge. From the later nineteenth century until 2007 this was in other official hands but was then reclaimed. In March 2011, having been cleared of undergrowth, it was replanted with fruit trees as the 'Greenwich Park Orchard', for eventual limited public access.

Quick-Reference Gazetteer

PLEASE NOTE that the format of this booklet prevents the map showing the south-western boundary of the Site up Stockwell Street / Croom's Hill / Chesterfield Walk, and along the south end of the Park but the directions of points of interest along this route are shown.

All building names that are marked* are either private or have no general public access.

Although most of the features listed lie within the World Heritage Site, a few outside have been included for general interest.

The West Gate of the Old Royal Naval College

The entries are arranged in the following order:

Major Buildings
Riverfront
Greenwich Park
Greenwich Park Borders
Town Centre
Statues

MAJOR BUILDINGS, *see pp.24–35.*

❷ is now occupied by Trinity College of Music, ❸ ❹ ❺ ❻ by the University of Greenwich

OLD ROYAL NAVAL COLLEGE (formerly Greenwich Hospital), *see pp.24–35.*

❶ **West Gate**. Designed by Thomas Ripley, 1749–51. The celestial and terrestrial globes on the pillars commemorate Commodore Anson's circumnavigation of 1740–44 in the *Centurion*, his track originally being marked on the latter. The gate was much closer to the buildings until it was moved in 1850 when Philip Hardwick also built the East Gate on Park Row.

❷ **King Charles Court***. By Sir John Denham (?), John Webb, and Sir Christopher Wren, 1664–1700, with reconstruction by Nicholas Hawksmoor, John James, James Stuart and John Yenn, 1712–1815. The east range, the first wing of Charles II's proposed royal palace, was built by John Webb, 1664–69, and remodelled for the Royal Hospital by Sir Christopher Wren and Nicholas Hawksmoor, 1696–1707. The west range was built by John Yenn, 1812–15, replacing the building of 1696–1704 by Wren, the north-end pavilion by Hawksmoor, 1712–15, and the south-end pavilion by James Stuart. Joshua Marshall's carvings in the east pediment show the Royal Stuart arms supported by figures of Fortitude and Dominion of the Seas, which, in the north, the same arms are supported by Mars and Fame.

❸ **King William Court** (* except Painted Hall). Designed and begun by Wren and finished under the direction of Hawksmoor and Vanbrugh, 1698–1717. Sir James Thornhill decorated the Painted Hall ceiling 1708–12. The painting celebrates the triumph of Protestant peace, with William and Mary attended by the Virtues presenting the cap of liberty to Europe above the crouching figure of tyranny, in the form of Louis XIV of France. The Upper Hall decoration, 1718–25, shows Mary's sister Queen Anne and her husband, Prince George of Denmark, in the ceiling and the Royal family of George I presiding over Naval Victory, Peace and Plenty. In the colonnade pediment, visible from the Hall, an impressive Coade stone sculpture installed in 1813, designed by Benjamin West, commemorates the battles and death of Nelson. Hawksmoor's brilliantly idiosyncratic west dormitory range of 1701–28, exhibits dramatic manipulations of architectural scale set off with carved nautical motifs on the courtyard front.

4 **Queen Anne Court***. Built by Wren and Hawksmoor from 1699, this only achieved its final form in 1748 when Ripley completed the end pavilions. Hawksmoor's arcaded centrepiece of the east front of the base block, 1699–1705, is the most striking feature. A temporary chapel that he built between the ranges in 1707 appears on some prints and was removed in 1751. The early seventeenth-century undercroft of the Tudor palace survives beneath the western range of this block and the Collingwood Room above remains the size and shape of the original large Hospital wards.

5 **Queen Mary Court** (* except Chapel). The last of the four Courts, it was laid out by Wren but not built until 1735–51 by Thomas Ripley. Ripley's chapel interior burnt out in 1779 and its replacement is the late Greek-revival masterpiece of James Stuart assisted by William Newton, 1779–89. The altarpiece of 1789, showing St Paul surviving the bite of a viper, after being shipwrecked on Malta, is the only major painting by Sir Benjamin West PRA still in the location for which it was painted.

The Discover Greenwich Visitor Centre in the Pepys Building

6 **Former Dreadnought Seamen's Hospital***. This was originally the Greenwich Hospital Infirmary, built by James Stuart, 1764–68, with a freestanding ward added on the west side in 1808–10. It was partially rebuilt after a fire in 1811 and substantially modified by Joseph Kay in the 1830s and 1840s. The building was leased in 1870 to the (merchant) Seamen's Hospital Society to replace the hospital ship *Dreadnought*, formerly moored off Greenwich. It is now the Dreadnought Library of the University.

7 **Pepys Building**. Erected between 1874 and 1883, it was originally the Royal Naval College's fives and racquets courts, flanking an open central courtyard. The court was roofed over as an engineering laboratory around 1906. The building is mainly notable for its imposing river façade, inset with busts of British naval heroes. It now holds Discover Greenwich – the vistor centre for the World Heritage Site and Old Royal Naval College – the Greenwich Tourist Information Centre and the Old Brewery café-restaurant and bar *(see.p.96)*. The former Hospital stable block between the Pepys Building and the West Gate was built by Joseph Kay in 1836 and was at that time outside the Hospital grounds.

8 **Devonport House* and Hospital Burial Ground**. Built on the site of the burial ground by Sir Edwin Cooper, 1924–34, as a nursing home, this incorporates two-thirds of William Newton's Greenwich Hospital School building of 1783–84 as a rear wing. It is now partly a student residence

The Trafalgar Quarters

and partly a conference hotel. The cemetery was closed in 1857 but Ripley's officers' mausoleum of 1750 and some graves around it remain. Captain Hardy of the *Victory*, later Governor of the Hospital, 1834–39, is one of many distinguished officers buried in the vault. Nelson's servant, Tom Allen, lies in a marked grave nearby.

⑨ **Trafalgar Quarters***. Built by John Yenn 1813–15, these handsome brick and stone offices have the Hospital arms in Coade stone over the central bays, and matching lodges. The Hospital's finances and out-pensions were administered here. It was later part of the Royal Hospital School and is now again run by Greenwich Hospital as sheltered housing.

THE ROYAL MUSEUMS, GREENWICH (a title granted by HM The Queen from January 2012), comprise the **National Maritime Museum**, **Queen's House** and **Royal Observatory**.

⑩ **The Museum (NMM)**, *see pp. 56–71*. Architects responsible: Daniel Asher Alexander, 1807–11; Philip Charles Hardwick, 1861–62; Admiralty architects under Captain (later Sir) Andrew Clarke, 1872–73; Colonel Charles Pasley, 1876; A.J. Pitcher with Sir Edwin Lutyens, 1934–37; Rick Mather Architects and Building Design Partnership, 1997–99; C.F. Møller with Purcell Miller Tritton, 2009–11. Alexander added the Tuscan colonnades and flanking wings to the Queen's House from 1807 for the Royal Naval Asylum, which subsequently became the Royal Hospital School. Other additions up until 1876 included Neptune Hall, the 1873 gymnasium behind the powerful Doric north frontispiece. During the NMM conversion Lutyens inserted a top-lit vestibule commemorating the Museum's benefactor Sir James Caird into Alexander's west wing. The work in the 1990s removed the Neptune Hall, replacing it with a high-level glass roof that forms a much larger covered courtyard between the Alexander and Hardwick ranges. The Sammy Ofer Wing, finished in 2011, includes a new main entrance, changing the main public approach from the north to the south (Park) side.

⑪ **NMM Administration** (business visitors only*). Alexander's east wing of 1807–11, only finally adapted to

Museum use in 1950–51 after wartime occupation by the Admiralty. The eastern entrance from Park Vista was inserted in the 1930s.

⑫ **The Queen's House**, *see pp. 16–23.* Built by Inigo Jones for Queen Anne of Denmark and Queen Henrietta Maria, 1616–35, with additions in 1662. One of the most important buildings in British architectural history this displays works from the NMM's superb art collection. Begun as an addition to the brick sixteenth-century Palace of Greenwich it was originally an H-block with a central bridge over the old Deptford to Woolwich road. In 1662 the upper floor was altered to a fully connected square layout with balanced sets of 'king's side' and 'queen's side' rooms. The cubic galleried Hall, the dramatic Tulip Stairs, the plasterwork of the 1660s east and west bridge rooms, and the logia offering views over the Park and Observatory give a flavour of its past splendour.

The Queen's House

⑬ **The Royal Observatory**, *see pp. 36–47.* Flamsteed House, the oldest part, was designed by Sir Christopher Wren and built in 1675–76 on the foundations of the former Greenwich Castle/Duke Humphrey's Tower. Wren described it as 'for the observator's habitation and a little for pompe'. The Astronomers Royal lived as well as worked there, although the Octagon Room was more useful for 'pompe' than regular observation. John Flamsteed, the first Astronomer Royal (from 1675) set up a more utilitarian sextant and quadrant house in the garden, part of which survives. His successor Edmond Halley built an adjoining one extended westward by Board of Ordnance Engineers, 1749–1813, and Admiralty Engineers and Architects 1851–95, to form the present Meridian and Great Equatorial Buildings. Longitude 0°, as defined by the seventh Astronomer Royal, Sir George Airy, passes through the Meridian Building. The time-ball on the east turret of Flamsteed House has indicated Greenwich Mean Time since 1833 by dropping at 1 p.m. precisely: the present ball dates from 1919. The red terracotta Altazimuth Pavilion and South Building were designed by William Crisp, 1894–95, in a period of rapid expansion of scientific work. Since 2007 the South Building has been an Astronomy Centre, with modern astronomy displays and learning facilities, linked to the 120-seat Peter Harrison Planetarium under its bronze cone. This has a programme of both live and recorded shows. (Note. Free entry to Astronomy Centre: paid entry for the planetarium. Separate entry charge for Flamsteed House and the Meridian Courtyard.)

The Royal Observatory

RIVERFRONT

14 Five-Foot Walk. Granted by Greenwich Hospital in 1731 as a public right of way between the buildings and the river, the name comes from its original width. The river walk now extends east to the O2 and west to the new Greenwich Reach developments flanking Deptford Creek.

15 *Cutty Sark* and Cutty Sark Gardens, *see pp. 50–55.*
The last surviving tea clipper, *Cutty Sark* is also arguably the most famous and beautiful. She was also the fastest sailing ship of her time. Designed for the China tea run she was launched by Scott and Linton of Dumbarton in 1869, the year that the opening of the Suez Canal undermined this trade for sailing ships. Her fastest passages were made in the Australian wool trade, to which she turned after 1877. After a period in Portuguese ownership she became a moored training vessel before being brought into permanent dry-dock here in 1954. The ship reopens following a nearly £45-million restoration in 2012, which has also raised her over 10 feet (3 m) to convert the dock below into a dramatic new public space. Cutty Sark Gardens, an entirely modern space, was formerly filled by the riverfront Ship Hotel and surrounding buildings, destroyed in World War II.

16 Greenwich Foot Tunnel. Built by Alexander Binnie, London County Council, 1900–02, originally for workers from south of the river to reach the London Docks. It is well worth going through the tile-glazed tunnel for the classic 'Canaletto' view of Greenwich from Island Gardens on the other side (beside the next DLR station toward London).

17 Greenwich Pier. Originally constructed in 1836 for the growing steamer traffic and still a major route for visitors to Greenwich by the frequent boat services. The new Pier buildings, originally proposed in the 1990s, were only constructed in 2011–12, to modified designs by Conran & Partners.

18 Trafalgar Tavern. An elegant building by Joseph Kay, 1837 which replaced the old George Tavern at the east end of Five-Foot Walk. Dickens, who knew it well, set the wedding breakfast in *Our Mutual Friend* here: 'specimens of all the fishes that swim in the sea surely had swum their way to it'. Until 1883 it was noted for its 'political' whitebait dinners. After damage in World War II it was divided as housing but was restored in late-Georgian style to tavern use in 1968. Crane Street behind it continues the river walk eastward and takes its name from the crane and the wharf at which stone for building Greenwich Hospital was unloaded.

The Trafalgar Tavern

Trinity Hospital

19 Trinity Hospital* to Ballast Quay. On the river walk, Trinity Hospital is an almshouse founded in 1613 by Henry Howard, Earl of Northampton. The present 'Gothick' remodelling dates to 1812. Beyond the large Greenwich Power Station, 1902–10, Ballast Quay is an attractive river frontage of early nineteenth-century houses* including The Cutty Sark pub. The view east to Blackwall Point and the O2 takes in Enderby Wharf, the base from 1834 of that family's South Sea whaling fleet. Later a cable works, the first transatlantic cable, laid by the Great Eastern in 1866, was made there. From 2012 a cruise liner terminal will operate from Enderby Wharf.

GREENWICH PARK, *see pp. 77–83.* The best view over historic Greenwich, London and the O2 is from the Observatory ⑬ and Wolfe statue ㊵ in the centre of the Park.

⑳ **Anglo-Saxon barrow group**. Thirty-one of these survive, although there were probably more. They date from the sixth to eighth centuries AD. Several were opened in 1714 by the Park Keeper, and others in 1784. Beads cloth, human hair and flints were among the finds.

㉑ **Blackheath Gate Lodge***. Built by John Phipps, 1851–52, this is an early and robust example of of the Domestic Revival style by an obscure official architect. It was built to house the Park Keeper as part of a campaign of improvements to extend public access.

㉒ **St Mary's Lodge and Gate**. Built in 1807–08, the lodge is an early example of John Nash's work in the Office of Woods and Forests, before he became involved in Regent's Park. It is an Italianate version of the picturesque estate lodge, designed to be seen at the end of a long downhill vista. Built as the Underkeeper's Lodge, it is now a Park café and information centre. This and the nearby St Mary's Gate take their names from the church which stood by the latter until 1936.

St Mary's Gate

Greenwich Park

㉒ **Herb Garden** located beside St Mary's Lodge.

㉓ **Castle Hill Gardens**. No access to or from Observatory.

㉔ **Ha-Ha Walk**.

㉕ **Greenwich Park Orchard***. Originally a 'dwarf' (i.e. nursery) orchard attached to the Queen's House. It has recently been taken back into Park management and replanted as an orchard, but with only limited occasional access.

㉖ **Queen Elizabeth's Oak**. This twelfth-century oak, dead for over 100 years and now fallen, was associated with Henry VIII and Elizabeth I.

For park statues, see p. 95.

GREENWICH PARK BORDERS, *see pp. 77–83.*

㉗ **Blackheath**. The assembly point of Wat Tyler's and Jack Cade's rebellions (1381 and 1450) and the massacre of Cornish rebels in 1497 (commemorative plaque by Park gate). Wide open spaces for kite-flying. A main line station is in Blackheath village, 20 minutes walk from the Park.

Vanbrugh Castle

(28) **Vanbrugh Castle*** and **Maze Hill**. Vanbrugh Castle was built from 1718 by this architect, playwright and Wren's successor as Surveyor to Greenwich Hospital, who lived here to his death in 1726. Its medievalizing design is exceptional for its time and is still clear despite later additions. It is the only survivor of a group of houses he built here for members of his family. Nos 32–40 Maze Hill* were originally the infirmary of the Royal Naval Asylum, built by Daniel Alexander, 1807–12. They stand on the Hospital's first burial ground of 1707–47, of which the enclosing walls and the officers' mausoleum survive.

(25) **Park Vista**. This connects Maze Hill railway station and the National Maritime Museum (east side) and has attractive eighteenth and nineteenth-century houses*. By the Museum and Park gate the upper front wall of no. 35, The Chantry*, bears the arms of Henry VIII (replaced 1975). Although much of the building dates from 1800 and later, it incorporates sixteenth-century brickwork, the remains of outbuildings of the Tudor palace *(see pp 10–15)*. No. 34 and St Alfege's Vicarage are westward extensions of 1807–08 and 1829 by Daniel Alexander and Joseph Kay for officials of the Royal Naval Asylum and Greenwich Hospital. The Manor House, no. 13*, is an attractive early 18th-century Georgian building with an unusual weather-boarded belvedere overlooking the Park.

(29) **Ranger's House**, Chesterfield Walk. Built *c.*1700–20 for Captain (later Admiral) Francis Hosier, it has a handsome front elevation of seven bays faced in red brick, with a tripartite frontispiece, doorways with Ionic columns and a Venetian window above. Isaac Ware added the south wing for the 4th Earl of Chesterfield, statesman and author, who lived here in 1749–73. The north wing was added between 1783 and 1794. It was official home of the Ranger of Greenwich Park from 1815, hence the name. The post was held from 1799 to 1812 by the estranged wife of George IV, Princess (later Queen) Caroline, who lived at Montagu House just to the south. This was demolished in 1815, but a plaque and a sunken outdoor bath inside the Park mark the site. Another plaque commemorates Ignatius Sancho (*c.*1729–80), the black writer who was butler and valet

at Montagu House. A plaque on Ranger's House commemorates the residence of Chesterfield and Field Marshal Viscount Wolseley. A superb building, it is now in the care of English Heritage and holds the remarkable Wernher Collection of fine and decorative art formerly at Luton Hoo. This collection is particularly notable for its Italian Renaissance material.

30 **Macartney House***, Chesterfield Walk. Next to Ranger's House, this was the home of General Wolfe and his parents from 1752 (commemorative plaque on the Park side). It dates from the seventeenth century, with later extensions including by Sir John Soane, 1802. In a letter of 1751 Wolfe referred to it as 'the prettiest-situated house in England'.

31 **Croom's Hill**. Winding up by the Park from Greenwich to Chesterfield Walk and Blackheath, this is one of London's best historic streets. Some houses* date from the seventeenth century, some partly earlier, with later frontages. The 1672 Gazebo of The Grange, no. 52*, is a notable feature built for Sir William Hooker who lived here from 1665 and was both Sheriff and Lord Mayor of London. Park Hall*, just above it, was built by John James, 1724, who intended to live there but never did so: it is also said to have been the local home of Sir James Thornhill. Heath Gate House, no. 66*, red brick of about 1630, is the oldest in Greenwich, completed even before the Queen's House. Our Lady Star of the Sea, the neo-Gothic Catholic church of 1851, is the first major work of William Wardell, later an important architect in Australia. The chancel and chapel of St Joseph were decorated by A.W.N. Pugin and the Lady Chapel by E.W. Pugin. The Manor House*, below and opposite Macartney House, was built *c.*1695–1700 for Commodore Sir Robert Robinson, a Lieutenant-Governor of the Hospital, and is one of the finest of its type and period in London. At the Greenwich end the Poet Laureate, C. Day-Lewis, lived at no. 6*.

32 **Fan Museum**, 12 Croom's Hill. Occupying two houses in a fine and well-restored row of 1718–21, this is the world's only museum on the history of fans, exhibiting an important private collection. It includes displays, workshops, an Orangery and a garden to the rear.

The Fan Museum

The Spread Eagle

33 **Spread Eagle Yard**. The Eagle was an eighteenth-century coaching inn when the corner on which it stands on Nevada Street (formerly Silver Street) was on the main road east out of Greenwich. The archway into the vanished stable yard was built about 1780 when the name of the inn, now a restaurant and café, also 'spread'.

TOWN CENTRE

㉞ **St Alfege's Church**.
The architect of the parish church, the first of 'fifty new churches' ordered under Queen Anne, was Nicholas Hawksmoor, 1711–14, with the tower designed by John James, 1730. The interior (restored after war damage) has memorials to General Wolfe, the Elizabethan composer Thomas Tallis, and the founder of the National Gallery, J.J. Angerstein. All are buried here, Tallis in the former church which collapsed in 1710. Alfege, Archbishop of Canterbury, was murdered on the site in 1012 by Danish raiders camped at Greenwich and the church has seen considerable restoration to mark the 1,000th anniversary in 2012.

㉟ **Greenwich Market**, Nelson Road and College Approach (Joseph Kay, 1829–49). This well-planned late-Georgian redesign of the town centre was the main part of improvements carried out for Greenwich Hospital (which still owns most of it). Its formal, symmetrical, stuccoed terraces were substantially complete by 1831, although the north side of College Approach (originally Clarence Street) came later. It compares favourably with contemporary schemes in central London. The glass market roof added in 1908 now makes it a lively all-weather space for craft stalls. The 1950s buildings facing in from east and west, now holding shops, were originally lock-up units for a fruit and vegetable wholesale market and will be replaced in 2013–14. Kay's fine pillared archway to College Approach still bears the sign 'A False Balance is Abomination to the Lord, but a Just

St Alfege's Church

Greenwich Market

Weight is his Delight'. Above it the Royal Clarence Music Hall operated for much of the nineteenth century. Attractive Turnpin Lane, at the south end of the Market, preserves a medieval street line, with a central arch through to the Nelson Road shopping parade.

Weekend Market

㊱ **Greenwich Church Street**. On the western side near St Alfege's, nos. 15–21 are a group of modest houses with shops of about 1700, nos. 19 and 21 originally being one building. Nos. 15 and 17 are the taller and apparently earlier pair. Such late Stuart or early Georgian buildings are now very rare. Dr Johnson, the great English literary figure of the early to mid-eighteenth century lived in Church Street after he first came to London in 1736.

㊲ **Greenwich Railway Station**. The London and Greenwich Railway was the world's first suburban line, built in 1836–38. It runs from London Bridge on a viaduct that may be the world's largest solid brick structure and, incidentally, gives a fine view of Thomas Archer's wonderful church of St Paul's Deptford which, like St Alfege's, was one of Queen Anne's 'fifty new churches'. The handsome station, built by George Smith in 1840, and rebuilt in 1878, originally had a high-level platform, lowered when the line was put in a cut-and-cover tunnel to run east beyond Greenwich in 1878. It is now also a DLR interchange.

STATUE POSITIONS

⑦ **Sir Walter Ralegh** (1554–1618); bronze, by William McMillan. Moved from Whitehall in 2001.
⑱ **Lord Nelson** (1758–1805); bronze, by Leslie Pover, 2005. Outside the Trafalgar Tavern.
㊳ **George II**, (r. 1727–60); by John Michael Rysbrack, 1735. Carved at the expense of Admiral Sir John Jennings, Governor of the Hospital, from a block of marble captured from the French.
㊴ **William IV**, 'The Sailor King' (r. 1830–37); granite, by Samuel Nixon, 1844. Moved from King William Street, London Bridge, in 1936.
㊵ **Major-General James Wolfe** 'of Quebec' (1727–59); bronze, by Robert Tait McKenzie. Gift of the Canadian people,1930.
㊶ **Captain Cook** (1728–79); bronze, by Anthony Stones, 1994. On the Park side of the Museum at the Jubilee Walk gate.
⑳ **Standing Figure, Knife Edge**; bronze, by Henry Moore RA, 1976. On hill near Anglo-Saxon barrows.

Captain Cook (1728–79)

Information for Visitors

Discover Greenwich and the Greenwich Tourist information Centre are in the Pepys Building (7 on the map) of the Old Royal Naval College. Discover Greenwich is the interpretation centre for the Maritime Greenwich World Heritage Site (visitgreenwich.org.uk) and presents an engaging overview to help visitors choose what they want to explore for themselves. The Greenwich TIC is linked to it adjacent to Cutty Sark Gardens. On the other side is the Old Brewery café-restaurant (open 10 a.m. – 11 p.m.) which incorporates a micro-brewery.

This guidebook is regularly updated but please note that museum displays mentioned in it, and other visitor information, are liable to change during its period of use.

RECREATION FACILITIES

42 **Weekend Market**. Antique and other stalls next to Greenwich Picture House.
42 **Greenwich Picture House**. Three screens, adjacent to the town centre hotel.
43 **Greenwich Theatre**. Formerly a Victorian music hall, attached to the Rose and Crown pub here. Part of its 1885 façade survives on Nevada Street.
44 **River Walk**, east to **O2**, west to Greenwich Reach and Deptford.
45 **Arches Leisure Centre**. Modern indoor swimming pools and sports facilities in an interesting building of 1928.
46 **Boating Pond**. Summer only.
47 **O2**. Major event arena and entertainment complex. River access from Greenwich Pier DLR/ Jubilee Line to North Greenwich, or buses.

World Heritage Site boundary

REFRESHMENTS (Park area only)

3 **King William Restaurant**
7 **Old Brewery**
10 **Paul Bakery**
10 **Museum Café**
10 **16 Seconds West Brasserie**
13 **Astronomy Café**
22 **Cow and Coffee Bean Café**
48 **The Pavilion Tea House**

TRANSPORT

17 **Thames Clipper Service**
37 **Greenwich Rail Station**
49 **Maze Hill Rail Station**
50 **London City Airport**
DR **Docklands Light Railway**

GENERAL

i **Greenwich Tourist Information Centre**. Tel: 0870 608 2000
C **Children's Play Area**
P **Parking**. Limited in Greenwich and tightly controlled, weekends included.
WC **Public Toilets** with ♿ (except King William Walk). Other toilets are in 'Discover Greenwich' (Pepys Building) behind Greenwich Pier.

VISITOR INFORMATION

General visitor enquiries, contact:
Greenwich Tourist Information Centre
2 Cutty Sark Gardens
Greenwich
London SE10 9LW
Tel: 0870 608 2000
E-mail: tic@greenwich.gov.uk
www.visitgreenwich.org.uk

For Old Royal Naval College enquiries, contact:
Greenwich Foundation for the Old Royal Naval College
2 Cutty Sark Gardens
Greenwich
London SE10 9LW
Tel: 020 8269 4747
E-mail: info@ornc.org
www.oldroyalnavalcollege.org

For all Royal Museums Greenwich enquiries, contact:
National Maritime Museum
Greenwich, London SE10 9NF
Telephone: 020 8858 4422
Recorded information:
020 8312 6565
www.nmm.ac.uk